THE REAL FACTS ABOUT
ETHIOPIA

by

J. A. ROGERS

Author of

"From Superman To Man,"
"World's Greatest Men and Women of African Descent," etc.

978-1-63923-065-5

Printed August, 2021

Cover Art By: Paul Amid

Published and Distributed By:
Lushena Books
607 Country Club Drive, Unit E
Bensenville, IL 60106
www.lushenabks.com

ISBN: 978-1-63923-065-5

Printed in the United States of America

Editor's Note

The Real Facts About Ethiopia was first written and published by J.A. Rogers in 1936. The 1982 edition was reprinted from a copy in the Special Collection of The Atlanta University Center, Robert W. Woodruff Library. We would like to thank the Special Collection Librarian, Ms. Gloria Mims for her assistance in making this copy available.

FOREWORD

"The chief danger to the white man arises from his arrogant contempt for other races, a contempt which in America is mixed with fear and hate and which has provoked fear and hatred in return. Europeans have recently enjoyed a fair advantage over their rivals which they have abused without the slightest regard for justice and fair play. This advantage will not be theirs in the future."—Dean Inge (The White Man and his Rivals.)

"You are forcing on the world the coming struggle between Asia, all Asia against Europe and America . . . You are heaping up material for . . . a gigantic Day of Reckoning . . . You are deaf to the voice of reason and fairness and so you will be taught with the whirling swish of the sword when it is red."—Achmed Abdullah.

For the past four centuries the European, or white race, has been colonizing in all the lands of the darker races. Thanks to its superior developments in death-dealing implements and the marked difference in the color of its skin it was enabled to set itself off as a superior race and to indulge in a orgy of plunder, murder, and extermination. This happening in the very lands of the colored peoples wounded their pride, aroused their deepest hate, and created in the hearts of darker peoples, totally unknown to one another, a common hostility to white peoples.

For centuries this animosity slumbered like a volcano, bursting at times into revenge as in the attacks on missionaries; the Indian Mutiny; or the Zulu uprising. Then two events came to arouse a unifying consciousness —black Ethiopia's defeat of white Italy in 1896, and colored Japan's victory over white Russia in 1905.

The growing resentment of the darker races against white supremacy stirred the far-seeing thinkers. White writers, hostile to the darker peoples as Putnam Weale, J. W. Gregory, Lothrop Stoddard, and Maurice Muret, and others friendly to them as Sir Harry Johnston, Jean Finot, Dean Inge and Sir Leo Money saw a conflict and even a war between the races. Colored writers as Achmed Abdullah of Afghanistan and W. E. B. DuBois of America have foreseen the same.

Whether this prediction will come true remains to be seen. But in this threat of Italy against Ethiopia another and very definite stage of colored opposition to white injustice has been reached. In this unjustified aggression against the last stronghold of black civilization the darker peoples of the world see a challenge to their very existence.

These darker races outnumber the white four to one. Two of the three foremost nations of the world, Britain and France, are almost wholly dependent upon the co-operation of their colored subjects. Of the 500,000,-000 people in the British Empire, 430,000,000 are colored. In the French empire 125,000,000 of the 170,000,000 are.

Of the 160,000,000 inhabitants of Africa, less than 3,000,000 are white. The sentiment of the white, or near-white North African, is anti-white and distinctly African. The blacks of Africa outnumber the whites 60 to 1, and in some sections a hundred to one.

From the poison of this universal color-line Britain will suffer the worst effect. This seems only just as she has been the first, the chief, and the strongest builder of the color-line. So firmly did Britain lay the foundations of this evil in the American colonies that centuries later it still defies all attacks of intelligence, commonsense, and humanity. So thoroughly did Britain teach her offspring, the United States, the lesson of racial discrimination and exploitation that the United States with her lynchings and burnings-alive of black people, was, prior to Mussolini's threat against Ethiopia, the foremost agent in keeping alive the resentment of the colored races against the white—the foremost in keeping open the old wounds of race hate.

A war in Africa, whichever way it goes, will be disastrous to Britain. If Ethiopia wins it will stir the pride of the African and urge him to oust the whites; if Ethiopia loses it will stir revenge and the effect will be the same. The 320,000,000 dark-skinned people of India will be similarly affected, now or later.

Whatever be the outcome of the threatened Italian aggression against Ethiopia the world consciousness of the darker races against white exploitation has been intensified and will not subside. As General Hertzog has said it seems that a deeper and more cruel era of hate, ill-will, and war than the world has even known is about to begin. The avalanche is on its way and it will not stop until the last vestiges of the brutal and debasing color-line imposed on the world by the white race shall have been shattered into irretrievable fragments.

One hears much about a union of English-speaking peoples to ensure world peace and brotherhood. The first step towards any such goal would have to be a union of Britain and America to wipe out their cruel color-line. Unless they do this, there will never be any peace until they meet the inevitable end of the unjust and oppressive nations.

We want no more wars, economic or racial. End color discrimination.

Gregory, J. W. Menace of Color. Phila., 1925.

Inge, Dean. Quar. Review. April, 1921.

Stoddard, Lothrop. Rising Tide of Color Against White World Supremacy. N. Y., 1920.

DuBois, W. E. B. Darkwater. N. Y., 1920.

Maurice Muret. Twilight of the White Races., N. Y., 1926.

Money, Sir Leo. The Peril of the White. London, 1925.

Spengler, O. The Decline of the West.

Abdullah, Achmed. Forum, Vol. 52, p. 484-497.

Ellis, W. Inviting a War of the Races. Overland Monthly.

Finot, Jean. Race Prejudice.

OF WHAT RACE ARE THE ETHIOPIANS ?

ECAUSE of the increasing importance of the Ethiopians in world affairs, certain writers, inspired no doubt by their old prejudice against the Aframericans, are widely denying that there is any racial relationship whatever between Ethiopian and Aframerican. The Ethiopians, according to these writers, are "Semitic," "Hamitic," "Caucasian," "without a single drop of Negro blood," etc., etc.

Now as regards the word "Negro" there are two interpretations, which are widely different, namely, the American and the universal. In the United States one as fair as a Scandinavian may be socially and legally a "Negro." Further, a black man who speaks with a foreign accent, wears a turban, or is of another nationality may be told that he is not a "Negro." For instance, there was the case of Dr. Hubert Harrison, a distinguished native of the Virgin Islands. Dr. Harrison was a full-blooded Negro if ever there was one. When, however, he applied for naturalization papers, he was set down by the authorities as "White." Harrison was Danish and in the ethnological omniscience of the State Department Danes are white, hence Harrison though coal-black was a white man. This writer saw the papers. The same was true of another light-colored Negro from Jamaica,

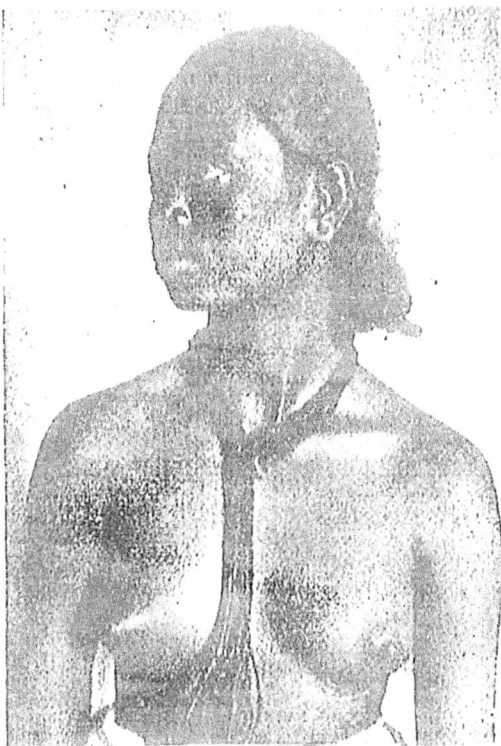

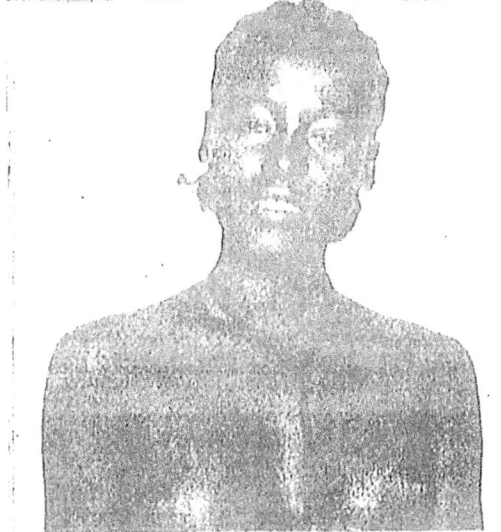

Some of the Ethiopian racial types. Lowest right is the type that is called Baria or Negro, in Ethiopia and the Near East. (Photo by the Author).

West Indies, whose papers were filled in thus: "Color, white; complexion, brown." Negro Porto Ricans are also set down as White.

In short, "Negro" in the United States is sometimes caste, sometimes race, sometimes both. Really to be able to define what is a Negro a scrambled brain is the first essential. And a touch of lunacy qualifies one as an expert.

In other lands, however, a Negro is usually an unmixed black man with wooly hair, thick lips, etc.

In the Orient, on the other hand, one drop of high-caste "blood" makes one high caste. It is culture, not color that counts. Africans, who come from the interior are of cruder culture and are looked down on much as in our lands, country-folks are. But from the days of the Pharaohs Negroes - from the interior who had the ability and the power, suffered little handicap. Many rose even to be rulers, one of the most conspicuous examples being Kafur.

"White" and "Negro," it must be remembered, are English. Their application to peoples of native African and Arabian descent is, therefore, an attempt by the English-speaking to denote social status. But since Orientals think not so much in terms of race as in terms of the social standing of the individual and that also of his tribe or nationality, color designations as "White" and "Negro" are almost meaningless to them. In Cairo, Egypt, the writer once saw a man of the deepest shade of ebony, with short, wooly hair and a Grecian nose. A dragoman, or guide, who was about three-fourths Negro, and was a Bedouin, told him that the man was a Negro; that his parents held others like him as slaves in Arabia, and that he, himself was not a Negro. Others, when questioned, confirmed this. Tippoo Tip, first ruler of the Belgian Congo, for instance, was known as an Arab, that is, a White man, but to all appearances, he was a full-blooded Negro. Much the same is true in Latin-American countries especially Brazil, where even dark mulattoes are classed as White. In short, in the Orient and Latin America wealth and social position, not color or hair, often determines "race."

In this sense then certain Ethiopian peoples as the Somali, Amharas, Tigreans, Shoans, who show some White admixture, would not be Negroes; only those like the Chankalla and the Yumbos, who show none would be.

If, however, we use the American definition of Negro, which includes all the shades from black to light-yellow and white, and all textures of hair from silky blond to tightly-curled wool, then every Ethiopian this writer has ever seen would be a "Negro" and nearer to the "pure" type than the average Aframerican.

The writer affirms this after having observed the Negroid type for thirty years in all its manifestations, and after having seen Negroes of nearly every nationality on the five continents—French, American, English, Portuguese, German, Australian, Egyptian, Sudanese, Haitian, Brazilian, Arabian, West Indian, etc., etc.

Some Somalis have straight black hair, but so have many Aframericans of Indian descent. Besides the Somalis would be uniformly darker. In short, even in the most learned and scientific circles there has never been any agreement as to what is a Negro. Writers like Elliot-Smith, Lady Lugard, and Dr. Junker have their definition of Negro; others equally informed as Sir Harry Johnston, Jean Finot, and Prof Dorsey, theirs, also.

As for Hamitic that is only a dark mulatto type which has become fixed by inter-breeding. A "son of Ham" has always been supposed to be a black man. It would be easy to pick out any number of what the scientists call Hamitic from among the mulattoes of the United States and

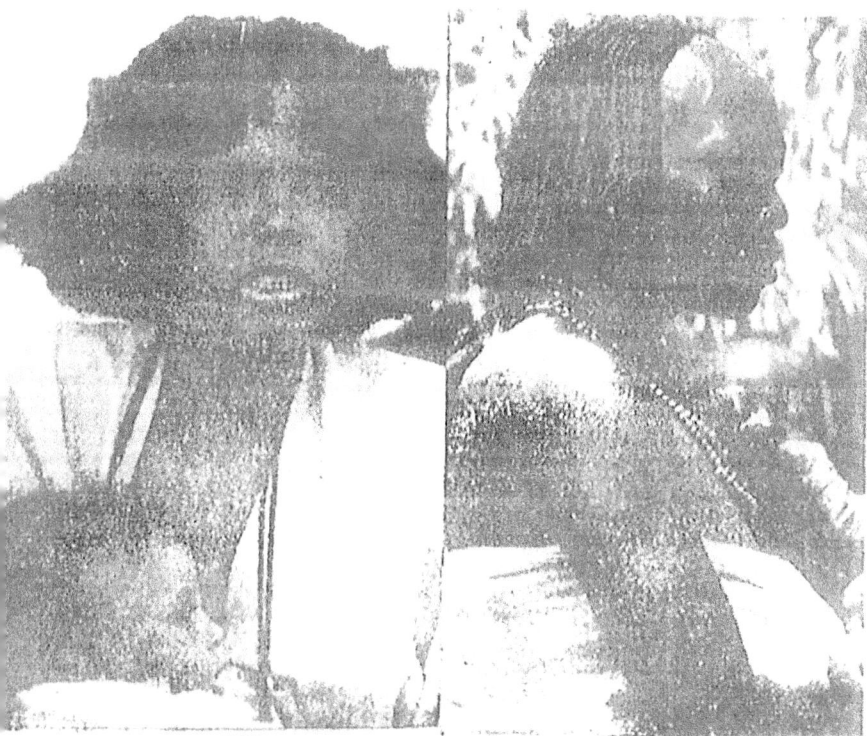

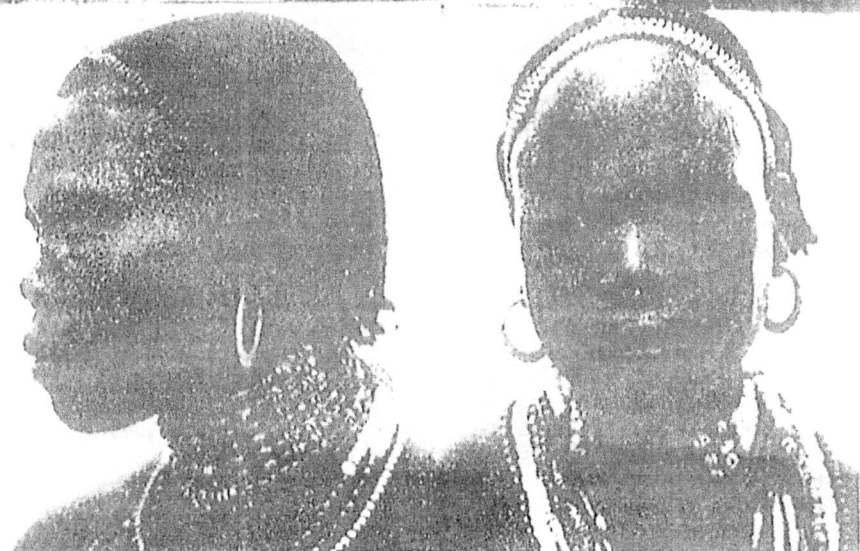

Above: Two Ethiopian mothers.   Below: Two Ethiopian belles.

the West Indies. This was the type that seemed to have predominated in Ancient Egypt and still does in modern one.

In reality there are only two varieties of mankind, the black and the white. All the others, as the Mongolian and the Indian, are in between. This is a commonsense view. But in ethnology, as in phrenology and theology, there is need for a mass of mystifying names in order to impress the uninformed.

As regards the Asiatic origin of the Ethiopians, it appears that a people known as the Habesha, migrated to Ethiopia from Yemen, Arabia. Some writers are insisting therefore that the Ethiopians are Asiatics. But that was before the Christian era. White people have been living in the New World only five centuries. Does one still call the descendants of Europeans in America, European?

Further the Yemenites are not only Negroid but it appears that all the present inhabitants of Africa, save the pigmies, originated in Asia.

As for the Semitic origin, there was a considerable migration of Jews to Ethiopia with Menelik I. But that was in 955 B. C. For the past 2,800 years these Semites have been mixing with the African natives until in some cases they are indistinguishable from them. Besides there was considerable Negro strain in the Jews in Solomon's time. Again the Falashas, a people of Jewish origin, still live in Ethiopia. They are black and unmistakably Negroid. Semitic, indicates language, not race. A Semite like an English-speaking person may be black or white.

Some white strain came into Ethiopia with the Portuguese and some has filtered in from Egypt, but not much.

The ruling classes of Ethiopians have mixed freely with the purer type Negroes. The masters have had children by these Negro women, and since there is no racial discrimination in Ethiopia the offspring also entered the ruling classes. Menelik II, the greatest of their rulers after Haile Selassie, was at least seven-eighths Negro.

"The Negro blood dominated in him (Menelik) as it did in many other Ethiopian chiefs" (I. L. Blanchot, Geographie, Dec. 1920, p. 451).

"Menelik's mother was a woman of low origin * * * giving him the Negroid face" (National Georgraphic Magazine, Vol. XII, p. 94).

As regards Haile Selassie, W. Alexander Powell, an American traveler, tells of a white American woman, who, when she saw him riding in state in Paris with Premier Poincare on the Champs-Elysees and later in the movies being entertained by King George, King Albert, and King Victor Emmanuel, wanted to know why all this fuss was being made "over a common African nigger."

"Yet," adds Powell, "the dusky little man who drove through the Paris streets . . . far from being a Negro is of blood as purely Caucasian as that of the American woman . . . " (Beyond the Utmost Purple Rim, p. 292).

Col. Powell thus sees Haile Selassie as a white man. But let us suppose that instead of being a guest of the Emperor, Powell had seen him riding incognito in a Pullman car or eating in an American restaurant, what would have been his feelings? From the Negrophobic tone of his book it is safe to say that they would have been the same as those of the white woman he rebuked.

Pictures of the Ethiopians that have been appearing in the newsreels and the newspapers fully confirm moreover what has been said of their Negroid strain. The more accurate news writers are doing the same. An Associated Press dispatch says "Hundreds of Ethiopian boys looking like Southern pickaninnies . . . strutted alongside bearded septugenarians who might have stepped from the pages of 'Uncle Tom's Cabin' " (N. Y. Post,

Aug. 21, 1935). In short, Africans are generally Negroid, as Eastern Asiatics are Mongoloid, and Europeans, Caucasoid.

Certain Ethiopian individuals who are eager for "white" culture would no doubt be proud if called white as certain mulattoes in the West Indies and South America would be, but the majority would be just as much displeased as the average white Southerner would be if called a Negro. The principal reason is that they know that the white man, or the red man, as they call him, covets their country.

This difference must be noted however. The Ethiopians have never drawn a color-line against white peoples.

For list of authorities on the Negro strain in the Jews, ancient and modern, consult "Jews and Ethiopians" in Rogers, J. A. "100 Amazing Facts About the Negro," with "The Key."

GENERAL HISTORY OF ETHIOPIA

ETHIOPIAN history goes so far into the past that what is said of its beginnings cannot be proved. But neither can it be disproved.

The name of its founder, according to the most reliable records, was Cush. The date of its founding is set at 6280 B. C., which is three times as long as from the birth of Christ to the present time, or a total of 8,200 years.

It had two capitals, Napata and Meroe, whose mighty ruins still stand. Ethiopia was known to the Egyptians as the land of Ksh (Cush). The word, Ethiopia, like the word, Egypt, is of Greek origin and came into use much later. The Egyptians called their land, Khemi. The Ethiopians probably called themselves Nubians.

This part of Ethiopia is now in the Anglo-Egyptian Sudan.

Another Ethiopia also extended to the south-east on the Red Sea. This was Habashat—the Abaseni (Abyssinia) of the Greeks—and was a part, or a province, of the first. It might even have been its mother-land. This part of Ethiopia was also founded by Cush, and its capital was Axum, whose relics also speak of a mighty past. Later these two Ethiopias seemed to have drifted apart for in the Fourth Century A. D. the Abyssinian Ethiopia invaded the Nubian one.

Ethiopia, in its earliest history included not only Africa but Southern Asia as far as India, according to Herodotus (525-484 B. C.). So-called Negro peoples predominated then in Asia Minor. Nimrod, the mighty hunter, a son of Cush, was founder of the Assyrian Empire. In Southern Arabia, Southern India, Siam, as far as Australia, and the islands of the Pacific, the Negroid type prevailed, and still does. Prof. Dorsey, one of the foremost and most realistic of the modern anthropologists says, "Wherever the Indian Ocean touches land it finds dark-skinned people with strong developed jaws, relatively long arms, and kinky or frizzly hair. Call that the Indian Ocean, or Negroid division of the human race" (Why We Behave Like Human Beings, p. 44.)

Ethiopia was generally believed by the most ancient scholars to have been the first of the nations and the mother of civilization. Modern scholars, basing their opinion on excavations, generally deny this. But since much is yet undiscovered, and since the ancient scholars were nearer the event, it seems logical to give them the benefit of the doubt until such time as the modern scholars have filled the gaps in their records.

Further, it is not unlikely that civilization might have come from the Ethiopians of Asia rather than from those of Africa?

In any case there is at least one proved connection between the two Ethiopias, namely, the written language of modern Ethiopia, or Ghez, is derived from the Meroitic, or ancient Ethiopian.

There can be no doubt as to racial identity of Ethiopians. Their monuments show them to be what we call Negroes today. The Encyldpedia Britannica says of these monuments, "The figures are obese, especially the women, and have the pronounced Negro features, and the royal person is loaded with bulging golden ornaments." Prof. Breasted particularly notes the Negroid features of one of the greatest of the Ethiopian rulers, Taharka, or Tirhaquah of the Bible.

Ethiopia was for a long time dominated by Egypt. But in 721 B. C. her king, Piankhi, conquered Egypt to the mouth of the Nile.

In 712 B. C. Sabacon, son-in-law of Piankhi, established the XXV, or Ethiopian Dynasty in Egypt. Taharka, a nephew of Sabacon, extended Ethiopian mastery in Assyria, and for a time gave her world mastery; but defeated by the Assyrians he retreated up the Nile to the original Ethiopian domains.

In 525 B. C. Cambyses, the Persian king, invaded Ethiopia and was repulsed by Nastasen.

The first king of Abyssinian Ethiopia was Ori, 4470 B. C. Haile Selassie I, is its 334th ruler. Modern Ethiopians have a connected list of their kings since Ori.

Ethiopia has been at war since the days of the Pharaohs. The chief reasons for this were that she owned the sources of the Nile and was rich in gold, which the Egyptians and others were ever striving for. After the Egyptians came the Mohammedans who from the seventh to the nineteenth centuries warred with Ethiopia for the same reason. It is these centuries of war with Islam which is probably the chief cause for the backwardness of Ethiopia among the nations today.

OTHER HIGHLIGHTS OF ETHIOPIAN HISTORY
Nubia or Cushite Ethiopia

1270 B. C. Memmon, King of Ethiopia, left Susa, his capital in Persia, with an army of 200,000 men (half white, and half black) to go to the aid of his uncle, King Priam, in the famous Trojan War.

944 B. C. Zera, King of Ethiopia, invaded Egypt and Palestine with an army of 1,000,000 men (according to the Bible) and is beaten back by disease and the armies of Asa, King of Judea.

30 B. C. The Romans invaded Ethiopia, and destroyed the capital, Napata.

20 B. C. Candace III, ruler of Ethiopia, invaded Egypt and pillaged Thebes.

Habashat, or Sheban, or Abyssinian Ethiopia

981 B. C. Makeda, Queen of Sheba, visited King Solomon in Judea.

955 B. C. Their son, Menelik mounted the throne of Ethiopia.

70 A. D. Juda, the eunuch of Candace, baptised by the Apostle Philip.

70 A. D. Candace established Christianity at her capital, Axum, making Ethiopia the first Christian nation.

341 A. D. Christianity restored in Ethiopia by Abraha and St. Frumentius.

524 A. D. The Ethiopians invaded Arabia and captured Yemen from the Jews.

569. The Ethiopians attacked Mecca and are repulsed. From this event started a world war that lasted more than a thousand years.

601. The Ethiopians were driven back across the Red Sea, later to lose all their coast-line to the Mohammedans.

937. Judith, Queen of the Falashas, or Black Jews, seized the Ethiopian throne and ruled 40 years.

977. Tekla Haimanot, Ethiopian saint, overthrew the Black Jews and restored the dynasty of Solomon and the Queen of Sheba.

1192. King Lalibala built the famous rock temples of Lasta, and invaded Arabia.

1434. King Zara Jacob sent envoys to the Council of Florence, Italy.

1442. Pedro de Covilham, envoy of John II, king of Portugal, visited Eskender II, king of Ethiopia.

1529. The war of centuries between Ethiopia and Islam continued. The terrible Mohammedan general, Mohammed-Gerad, invaded Ethiopia.

1544. The Ethiopians, aided by the Portuguese, routed the Mohammedans and killed Mohammed-Gerad.

1649. King Fasildas drove the Portuguese from Ethiopia.

1843. Sahle-Selassie, "The Great," made a treaty with France.

1867. A British army, 15,000 strong, invaded Ethiopia to free white missionaries.

1889. The Mahdists, 40,000 strong, are repulsed with terrible slaughter by King John. This practically marked the close of 1,100 years of the Mohammedan attempt to seize Ethiopia.

1896. Menelik defeated the Italians at Adowa.

1916. Battle of Sagalle. Lidj Yassue, Ethiopian Emperor, beaten by Haile Selassie. 20,000 slain. Zaiditu placed on the throne.

1923. Ethiopia entered the League of Nations.

1930. Haile Selassie crowned Emperor.

1934. Armed conflict for possession of the oasis of Walwal in Ethiopia started the great Italo-Ethiopian quarrel.

BOOKS ON ETHIOPIAN HISTORY

Budge, Sir E. A. W. The History of Ethiopia. 2 vols. London, 1928.
Budge, Sir E. A. W. The Egyptian Sudan. 2 vols. London, 1907.
Reisner, G. A. Excavations at Nuria—The Kings of Ethiopia. Harvard African Studies. II. Varia Africana II.
Reisner, G. A. The Pyramids of Meroe and The Candaces of Ethiopia, in Museum of Fine Arts. Bull. Boston, Mass., April, 1923.
Morie, L. J. Histoire de l'Ethiopie, 2 vols., Paris, 1904.
Sellassie, G. Chronique du Regne de Menelik II. 2 vols, Paris, 1930 (The author is an Ethiopian).
Littman, E. Deutsche Axum-Expedition. 4 vols. Berlin, 1913.
The Catholic Encyclopedia (see Cush) vol. IV. p. 575.
    (All but Morie's are illustrated.)
Read also "Abraha Al-Arsham, Emperor of Yemen and Ethiopia" in "World's Greatest Men and Women of African Descent," by J. A. Rogers.
For additional facts and authorities on Ethiopians and their descent see also Rogers, J. A. 100 Amazing Facts About the Negro with "The Key."

THE STORY OF ITALIAN AGGRESSION AGAINST ETHIOPIA

TALY'S dealings with Ethiopia have been marked with trickery and coveteousness from the first. Whenever the Ethiopians outtricked the Italians, however, and this was often, it was charged to that spirit of treachery, thievery, and craftiness supposed to inhere in African peoples.

Let us review briefly the earlier history of this Italo-Ethiopian strife. It is highly necessary to an understanding of the present quarrel. Let us also remember, at the outset, that the two countries are 4,000 miles apart, and that the only Ethiopians who have ever tried to enter Italy are students, tourists and religious pilgrims.

In 1876, when that arch-murderer, voluptuary, and lover of good things to eat, Leopold II, King of the Belgians, took away the rich empire of the Congo from its owner, Tippoo Tib, an Arab Negro, he started a rush of the European powers that in less than 30 years took away nearly all of Africa from its original owners.

At that time Italy was too exhausted from her long struggle for independence against Austria and the Pope to reach out for any. In 1869 when the Suez Canal was opened, however, the Rubattino Steamship Company, an Italian concern, leased the port of Assab on the Red Sea from the Sultan of Raheita as a coaling station. In March, 1870, Rubattino bought the port outright for $9,440.

Ten years later, the Italian government, spurred by the rich loot being taken out of the so-called Dark Continent by Leopold and others, began to have African aspirations. She recalled the vast empire that Rome once held in Africa. Accordingly, she gave Rubattino $43,200 for Assab and placed it under her flag.

Most of the land along the Red Sea, though worthless for agriculture, is of high strategic value. It lies on the route to India, England's most prized possession. England, therefore, highly mistrustful of the entry of any other power in this region, made strong protest. So did Egypt and Turkey, who owned territory there. It is notable that at this time the only friend that Italy had in East Africa was Ethiopia. Finally, after much negotiation, British objections were overcome, and those of Egypt and Turkey ignored.

On July 5, 1882, Italy formally placed Assab under the Italian crown. This was the first colony she had had in Africa since the days of the Caesars.

With her appetite now whetted, Italy reached out for Massowah, a port with a rich trade with the interior, and Europe and Asia, since the time of Cleopatra. This time England was much more cordial. She was being beaten by the Mahdi, the great Negro prophet of the Soudan, and she welcomed another white power. Hence she permitted Italy to grab Massowah from Egypt. Encouraged, Italy continued to acquire territory along the Red Sea by tactics that are mostly dubious, until she had nearly 40,000 square miles. This she consolidated into the colony of Erithrea—45,374 square miles—in 1890.

While on the subject of Italian expansion in Africa, let us finish with it. Her next acquisition was in Somaliland, where she took under her flag 245,000 square miles, the greater part of which, 190,000 square miles,

Veterans of Adowa: Left, Menelik II; right, the Warrior Empress, Taitu. Center: The Ras Makonnen, father of Haile Selassie.

was ceded by England. For the remainder she paid $72,000 to the Sultan of Zanzibar.

Her next African grab was in her war with Turkey in 1911-12. From this Moslem power she took Tripoli—360,000 square miles—and Cyrenica—75,340. These were made into the Italian colony of Libya, with 580,000 square miles.

Italy in 30 years had acquired 870,534 square miles—a territory one-fourth the size of the United States and six times larger than herself. But here's the rub: This vast empire was mostly rocky, arid, broiling desert, and worth less than a few acres of suburban New York. At best it was a liability. This was why Italy had been permitted by the other powers to have it. England, as was said, gave Italy most of the Somaliland territory, and when Britain cedes any territory you may be sure it is absolutely worthless and a burden.

But there was method in Italy's madness. Count Crispi, the Mussolini of 1894, saw again a great Italian empire stretching from Tunis across the way from Sicily to down the entire length of the Red Sea. Two of these worthless colonies, Erithrea and Somaliland touched Ethiopia, the first on the northeast, the second on the southeast. Standing on his hot, barren rocks, the Roman Wolf now cast greedy eyes upwards to where his rich, fertile neighbor, Ethiopia, lay in the cool, well-watered mountains. Europe had grabbed all of Africa save this prize. He licked his chops greedily. He would finish the job.

Let's go back to 1885. Italy, having squatted to the northeast of Ethiopia made it clear that she meant to annex the ancient empire simply by marching in and taking it as England, France, Belgium and Portugal had done other parts of Africa.

At the time Ethiopia was being torn with civil war. John, son of Theodore, a usurper, was at war with Menelik II, the rightful heir. Agostini Depretis, the Mussolini of that day, seized the opportunity to invade Ethiopia and annexed a choice portion, adjoining Erithrea. It was Menelik's land, but the robbery made John uneasy. After Menelik had been eaten his turn would be next.

Leaving his rival, John, Menelik marched against the Italians. Several skirmishes followed with Menelik, sometimes the victor, sometimes the Italians. On Jan. 14, 1887, Menelik captured Count Salembini, who had penetrated into the interior on a supposed scientific mission, and held him as a pledge that the Italians would quit his territory. They refused.

The Ethiopians, commanded by the Ras Alula, thereupon marched against the Italians, whose forces consisted of 512 whites and several thousand natives, under Col. Cristofori. They met at Dogali on Jan. 26, 1887. Surrounded by the Ethiopians, the Italians were thoroughly defeated, the only survivors being eighty-two wounded. On this the remaining Italians in Ethiopia retreated to the coast leaving behind their supplies. The moment seemed favorable for the Ethiopians to push Italy from East Africa, but they contented themselves with occupying the strategic posts. For the release of Salembini, Menelik demanded and obtained the release of a large supply of ammunition that Italy had captured at sea.

The defeat at Dogali by a black nation aroused deep anger and humiliation in Italy. Depretis was driven from office. Italy, burning for revenge, voted $6,000,000 for the war and sent out 12,000 well-equipped white troops, a large army in those days. Supplemented with 13,000 black troops, the Italian commander, General San Marzano entered Ethiopia in December, 1887, determined to conquer it once for all. In February, 1888, he captured Saati and built a railroad linking it with Massowah. But when a clash seemed near, the Ethiopian army suddenly retreated. The reason was that their old foes, the Dervishes, or Mohammedans had invaded Ethiopia. The Italians, perhaps not knowing this and think ing it a trap, retreated to their territory also. But they returned in May 1888, and were defeated at Saganeiti. Again they quitted Ethiopian ter ritory.

These three failures made Italy realize why England and the other European powers hadn't gobbled Ethiopia. Britain, it is true, had invaded Ethiopia in 1867 as far as the mountain fortress of Magdala to punish the mad king, Theodore, for his seizure of English missionaries. This had been done, however, with the general consent of the Ethiopians and Britain had retired immediately taking with her some priceless Ethiopic manu-scripts, and the Kebra Nagast, or Ethiopian Book of Kings, which had first been written in 400 B. C.

The Italians now attempted to gain their ends by craft and diplomacy. John and Menelik, being still at war, they decided to play one against the other after the manner in which Cortez with a handful of men had seized Mexico. General Barateri, the Italian commander visited Menelik and offered him arms to regain the throne of his ancestors. Similar overtures were made to John. Both accepted but with little intention of keeping their promises. Italy complains bitterly of the lack of Ethiopian faith. The simple truth is that there has been no faith involved on either side. It was a case of ruse against ruse with the Africans being the trickier of the two.

John and Menelik thought themselves justified when they saw the Italians nibbling at their territory. Finally when Barateri permitted the pillaging of Adowa by native troops, Menelik realized that no confidence whatever could be placed in him. What the Italians did not know, more-over, was that their aggression had driven John and Menelik together and that the two had made a treaty, whereby Menelik should be John's heir. To bind the bargain, John's son, the Ras Area, married Menelik's daughter, Zaiditu, or Judidth.

Soon after John was killed in battle with the Mahdi, a Negro prophet, who had driven England from the Soudan. Ras Mangascha, John's son claimed the Ethiopian throne, and civil war broke out again.

Count Crispi, then Premier, saw his opportunity. Crispi's dream, like that of Mussolini's, was an African empire stretching from Sicily to the Straits of Babel-Mandeb and taking in Tunis, Egypt, the Soudan, and Ethiopia. Accordingly he took advantage of the disorder to march into Ethiopia. At the same time he sent a mission, headed by Count Antonelli, to hail Menelik as the rightful sovereign, and to make a treaty with him.

This treaty, known as Outchale in Ethiopian and Ucciali in Italian, was signed in 1889. By its terms Italy lent Ethiopia 4,000,000 gold francs ($800,000), a half of which was to be in arms and ammunition. As security Italy was given control of the customs at Harrar, a rich coffee province. In case of non-payment. Harrar was to be ceded to Italy. Menelik, pressed by Mangascha, accepted these severe terms. Two copies of the Treaty of Outchale, Ethiopia had pledged to make all negotiations

Italy, now triumphantly announced to the European powers that Ethiopia was her protectorate. King Humbert of Italy sent 38,000 rifles and 28 modern cannon to his new "son" Menelik, who replied with a slice of land, known as Asmara.

The next four years were peaceful, despite continued Italian aggression on Ethiopian territory. Italy justified herself by deciding that she was dealing with an "inferior" people.

About 1892, Menelik was seized with the ambition to modernize his country as the Japanese were doing. He instituted a postal service and struck coins and stamps with his own effigy. To this Italy strongly objected.

Then he started to make treaties with Germany, Russia and Turkey, on which Italy exploded in wrath. She said that according to the terms of the Treaty of Outchale, Ethiopia had pledged to make all negotiations with the other powers through her.

Menelik objected vigorously. He pointed to Art. 17 of the treaty with the Amharic word, "itchalloutchal," which means, "may, if he pleases," use Italian diplomacy. The Italians insisted that in their copy the word was "must", use Italian diplomacy. Menelik submitted the treaty to the leading Oriental scholars of Europe and Africa. They agreed that he was right and that he had not made his country a protectorate of Italy.

Apropos of this: On December 18, 1895, the Marquis du Rudini, ex-Premier, admitted in the Italian Parliament that Menelik was right (See; Revue Francaise et Exploration, vol. XXI, p. 30, 1896).

Menelik, eager to maintain his long friendship with King Humbert of Italy, wrote him.

"I realize that the Amharic text and the Italian version of this article 17 differ. But in signing it I stipulated that Ethiopian affairs could be treated by Italian diplomacy on my invitation. I have never promised to have it done by Italy alone.

"Your Majesty ought to understand that no independent power could ever make such a concession. If you have the honor of your ally, Ethiopia, at heart, you'll change this.'

Italy, realizing what it would mean to her prestige in Europe, if she yielded to this black, and as she deemed it, barbarian people, replied through her envoy.

"King Humbert cannot yield. It would hurt the pride and dignity of his people."

Menelik, with the thought of his country's seven thousand years of independence, flashed back, "If you have your dignity, so have we."

The Empress Taitu, warrior wife of Menelik, added, "You wish to make us your pupils but that will never be."

"Your Majesty," said the Italian envoy, "this means war."

"Then let it come," replied Menelik firmly. "We cannot permit our integrity as the oldest Christian nation to be questioned, nor the right to govern ourselves in absolute independence."

Menelik's first step was to return the amount of the loan with three times the stipulated interest. He took care, however, to keep the arms and ammunition that his estranged "brother," Humbert had given him.

Crispi at once made extensive preparations for the conquest of Ethiopia. His Parliament voted $8,000,000 for the war. At the same time he sent heavy shipments of arms to Mangascha and all the chiefs hostile to Menelik.

Italy, already beaten back three times, was cautious about attacking Menelik, however, and sent an envoy to him, asking him to yield. Menelik, like Haile Selassie, pledged to fight to the last man rather than surrender.

In this crisis Menelik now showed that statemanship, which has placed him among the foremost leaders of modern times. He had conquered the greater part of Ethiopia and had reduced the chiefs to his will. Many of them were still angry with him. But assembling his messengers he sent

Veterans of Adowa. Above, left to right, the Ras Michael, father of the ex-Emperor Lidj Yassu; Ras Mangascha, son of King John. Below: Hapti Giorgis, Minister of War; and the Ras Alula, Chief Commander at Adowa.

them over the land to all the kings and chiefs urging them to unite against a foe who was going to take from them even such measure of independence as they had enjoyed under him. Did they want to submit to the white man who had seized and enslaved all the rest of Africa? They assembled at Boromeda. Menelik addressed them in stirring language. "Whatever be our differences we can never permit our country which has maintained its freedom for seventy centuries to be ruled by an outsider. You have seen what the white man has done to the rest of Africa. Do you, a proud fighting race, want to be enslaved like the other inhabitants of this continent? Ethiopia has never been conquered. And she shall never be as long as she preserves her indomitable spirit. Ethiopia shall ˆstretch her hand only to God—and to smite her enemies."

All pledged their allegiance. The Ras Mangascha, Menelik's chief foe asked to be permitted to lead the attack. "I will drive out the Italians," he said, "with the very bullets they gave me to kill you."

Count Crispi now decided once for all on the conquest and annexation of Ethiopia, while England, France, Russia and Austria protested. Italy voted an additional $4,000,000 to carry on the war and sent out 15,000 more men.

To show his defiance, Crispi seized three Ethiopian princes who were studying engineering in Switzerland and held them as hostages over the protest of the Swiss.

Italy won at first. At Coatit and Senafe in 1895 she defeated Mangascha. Another victory at Delsa was telegraphed to Rome and magnified into a triumph. The war was already won!

But these successes were only a trap. Mangascha had been instructed to draw the enemy into the country away from his base, toward Menelik who was awaiting with 90,000 men.

On December 7, 1895, at Amba Alagi the advancing Italians, 5,200 strong, encountered the vanguard of the Ethiopian army which was commanded by the Ras Makonnen, and were killed to a man. Laying siege to the Italian stronghold at Makalle, Makonnen captured it, forced the Italians to pay $500,000, and to surrender all their arms.

The $500,000 had been paid for the ransom of the captured Italians. In returning these Menelik showed a strategy, which some military experts declare is without a parallel for shrewdness. He had the Ras Makonnen escort the prisoners to the Italian lines, at the same time giving the impression that he, himself, was going to attack Addigrat, another Italian post. But when half-way he changed his direction and marched on the main body of the Italian army. The first of these movements had served as a screen for the second and had completely fooled the Italian scouts.

Before Barateri was aware of it he found himself blocked by the main body of the Ethiopian army. Retreat was his only salvation. But since he could not be sure even of that he tried to make terms with Menelik. The latter demanded the payment of $12,000,000 and the evacuation of all Ethiopian territory.

For the next five weeks negotiations went on, while the two armies rested within eighteen miles of each other. The Italians had 20,521 men of whom 7,330 were natives, and 64 cannon. Menelik outnumbered them four to one. But his men had mostly spears. His 42 cannon were nearly all old style. The Ethiopians, great cavalry fighters—they were the first to use horses in warfare—had only 8,600 horses. A plague had killed nearly all their animals.

Faced with these conditions, Barateri telegraphed to Crispi making known his precarious position, and saying that should the enemy attack he hoped to be able to repulse him. But Crispi, who was faced by a similar crisis at home, and wished to re-instate himself by a coup, sent a stinging reply. He accused Barateri of suffering from "military rheumatism."

"Give me a decisive victory, or out you go," was his ultimatum.

On the night of February 29, 1896, Barateri took advantage of the moonlight and the fact that the next day was a great feast of the Ethiopians—that of St. George's—to advance.

Warned by his scouts, Menelik moved forward although a third of his men were away for the holiday. By using mountain passes unknown to the Italians he crept upon them and surrounded them almost entirely.

At 6:30 the next morning the Italians opened the battle. Their mountain guns played havoc with the massed Ethiopians. But Menelik, bringup his modern quick-firers replied with vigor. Then he gave the order to advance on all fronts, and the Ethiopians sweeping down, pressed the Italians into such a closely packed mass that they could not use their guns. Many of their cannon were found after the fight, unfired. Thereafter the battle was a massacre. The Ethiopians speared the foe like sheep. By 3:00 P. M. the Italians were in full flight, leaving 12,000 dead.

The Ethiopians did not pursue them but the black subjects of Italy, taking advantage of the defeat, slaughtered the fugitives.

Among the slain were two Italian generals, Dabormida and Arimondi. Albertone, a third, was captured with 7,000 men. The entire supplies, including the 56 cannon and 4,000,000 cartridges fell to Menelik, whose loss was between 3,000 and 5,000 slain.

The victory resounded around the world. It amazed Europe and heartened black men everywhere. Especially it gave to the oppressed Africans new hope.

There was a rush of the European powers to make treaties with Menelik. From being considered an insignficant barbarian, he became a figure of importance.

The Ras Alula, a really great commander, came in for high praise. Guglielmo Ferrero, an Italian, and one of Europe's leading historians, believes that Count Schiefflin, head of the German General Staff and author of the plan for the German offensive on Paris in 1914, endeavored to imitate Ras Alula's strategy at Adowa. Schiefflin credited it to Hannibal, says Ferrero, because Ras Alula was black and he did not wish to give credit to a black man (Hannibal, of course was also a Negro).

"The battle of Adowa," says Ferrero . . . "is a little known but brilliant case of surrounding on both wings . . . If we took Count Schiefflin's doctrines literally the greatest warrior in history would appear to be the Ras Alula, the general in command of the Abyssinian forces at Adowa. Ras Alula succeded where Napoleon and Hannibal had failed. With a Vernichtungslaat (a single drive) lasting one day the Ras Alula solved a vital problem for his country.

"Thanks to the battle of Adowa, the Ethiopian empire has lived for forty years unmolested by the imperialistic ambitions of the West" (N. Y. American, November, 1933).

In Italy the effect was terrific. Crispi was mobbed in Parliament by angry Italian mothers, and driven from office. Italian soldiers mutinied rather than go to Africa. When General Balciderra, the new Italian commander, declared that it would take an army of 250,000 men, $1,100,000,000, and five years to conquer Ethiopia, Italy was forced to recognize the absolute independence of Ethiopia and to pay an indemnity of 10,000,000 gold lira, which was then worth about $5,000,000.

Is it any wonder after these futile and costly attempts that Italy now shows such desperation in her efforts to grab Ethiopia. Of all the European nations she has had by far the worst luck in Africa. After this toll of lives and expenditure of money then and since her territory there is still almost worthless rock and burning sand.

On December 5, 1934, Italy resumed active aggression again. Walwal, where the present dispute began, is sixty miles within the Ethiopian border, even on the Italian maps. Italy now claims this as her territory asserting that Ethiopia has no well-defined borders. But a nation without them could not be admitted to the League. Count Bonin Longare, the Italian delegate, who sponsored Ethiopia's admission in 1923, when asked whether Ethiopia's borders were clearly marked, replied in the affirmative.

For full details of Ethiopia's admission into the League and the cordial attitude of Italy, then, as well as the discussion on slavery, see: League of Nations Official Journal, Special Supplement, No. 19, Geneva, 1923.

SLAVERY IN ETHIOPIA

LAVERY in one form or another exists in nearly all Africa today. It was only in 1928 that the slaves of Sierra Leone, Britain's oldest African colony, were finally freed, or were said to be.

In Ethiopia slavery goes back to the most ancient times. It was also sanctioned by Mosaic law which Ethiopia still uses.

The first slaves in Ethiopia, as elsewhere, were prisoners of war, who were unable to pay ransom. These slaves begat slave children. Ethiopia, nearly always at war, continued to accumulate slaves.

Since the Ethiopian is a warrior by profession he shuns other work, hence slaves were needed to till the soil. There has also been a demand for slaves in Arabia from time immemorial. It is held that but for this importation of human beings the Arabian population would become extinct. Today the majority of slaves imported into Arabia come from Ethiopia and the Sudan.

Ethiopian, and other Oriental slavery, differ widely from American slavery. It is domestic servitude. The slaves, far more often than not, became a member of the family. Slaves who have children by the master, are not only freed, but the children are treated in all respects like the legal ones. A son by a slave mother might in time become the head of the family. Many rulers of the Mohammedan empire even at the height of its power had slave mothers. Indeed these were preferred in order to avoid political meddling by her family. Sometimes these slave mothers were Ethiopian.

Menelik, the greatest of the Ethiopian emperors, prior to Haile Selassie, had a slave mother, named Edgig Ayeihu. Ethiopian slavery was never as degrading as American slavery.

Beginning with Theodore, succeeding Ethiopian emperors have tried to abolish slavery in vain. It was too ingrained. Moreover African conditions forced many individuals to seek masters in order to get food and protection. Others voluntarily went to Mecca as pilgrims in order to sell themselves.

When Haile Selassie became regent he took steps to wipe out slavery.

Above: Left to right, Hapti Michael, Chief Commander of the Ethiopian Army
(Photo by the author); and an Ethiopian grand dame. Below: Young Ethiopia.

It was, moreover, one of the conditions by which Ethiopia was admitted to the League. It was impossible, however, to bring about immediate emancipation because large numbers of the slaves had no homes. Turned adrift they would become either beggars or bandits. Many also refused to leave their masters.

Italy, herself, praised Haile Selassie for his fight against slavery when he had done far less than now. Count Bonin-Longare, Mussolini's delegate to the League of Nations, said: "One must, however, pay tribute, particularly to Ras Tafari (now Haile Selassie) present heir to the throne, a prince of broad views who is open to modern ideas and in whose praise one can mention the decree of November, 1918, reinforcing all previous edicts and punishing slave traffic severely.

"As regards the condition of the slaves, a gradual humanizing of habits of life has brought about an improvement in their position so that it is more appropriate to speak of serfs rather than of slaves."

The greatest evil of slavery is slave-raiding. Haile Selassie has fought this vigorously. He executes all slave-raiders caught. But Ethiopia has been no more successful against the boot-legging of slaves than the United States with all its power and wealth was against the liquor traffic.

Many Europeans are in collusion with the slave-traders. The greatest of the modern slave-dealers was a Frenchman. To reach Arabia, where slaves fetch a high price, one must pass through Italian, French or British territory. Ethiopia has no sea-coast. It means, therefore, that one or more of the European powers surrounding Ethiopia are lax about smuggling.

In 1935, Haile Selassie decreed a general emancipation, but slavery whether voluntary or forced will continue until there is an industrial change in Ethiopia.

Slavery cannnot be condoned even when it takes the disguised form of Fascism. But if we are inclined to be impatient with slavery in Ethiopia let us remember that although it was abolished in America seventy years ago that it survives as peonage in the United States today. Certain American States sell their prisoners to business concerns and pocket the money. And in order to get this revenue minor social misdemeanors of Negroes are magnified into offenses drawing heavy fine and imprisonment. Peonage in America is not only more harsh than slavery in Arabia and Ethiopia, but there is far less economic justification for it.

Finally a liberated Ethiopian slave becomes a man at once and loses the stigma of servitude. He may rise to a position inferior only to that of the emperor, as in the case of Hapti Giorgis, one of the greatest of the Ethiopian generals and a national hero. But in the United States the curse and the stigma of slavery is still visited on the great-great-grand-children of the ex-slaves.

———

For Haile Selassie's pronouncement on slavery and the decrees of the Ethiopian government respecting it see: League of Nations, series 6-B. No. 9, Geneva, May 14, 1924.

Kessell, J. Marches d'Esclaves. Paris.

Rutter, E. Holy Cities of Arabia. London, 1928.

Makin, W. J. Red Sea Nights. London, 1932.

Simon, Lady K. Slavery. London, 1929.

Slavery. League of Nations Publ. VI. B.1 1935.

For additional information on slavery and authorities see: Rogers -J. A. 100 Amazing Facts About the Negro and "The Key" (Slavery).

GEOGRAPHY, ECONOMIC CONDITIONS, ETC.

ETHIOPIA has an area of from 350,000 to 450,000 square miles, or larger than Italy, France and the State of New York combined. The population is estimated at from ten to twelve millions.

It is bordered, for the greater part, by desert, where the temperature reaches, in places, 150 degrees in the shade. In the uplands the climate ranges from a mild tropical to a semi-tropical, while some of the mountains are 15,000 feet and are snow-clad. Addis-Ababa, the capital, is 8,000 feet high. In the winter months the climate is heavenly with its bright sunshine and almost frosty nights.

Ethiopia is the most mountainous region in Africa with gorges perhaps deeper and vaster than any in the world. One of these, the Takasse, is larger than the Grand Canyon. Ethiopia's mountains have been her strength. She has been rightly called "The Switzerland of Africa."

There are many rivers, the largest of which is the Abai, or Blue Nile. Of the several large lakes, Tsana (not Tana) comes first with an area of 1,150 square miles. Two of these, Hora Abyata and Shala, are salt.

Ethiopia's natural resources are of the richest. First, at least in historical importance, is gold. It was the source of this metal for ancient Egypt. Its natives still wash gold in the same streams five thousand years later.

Western Ethiopia is rich in oil and so are parts of the eastern. There are also platinum, silver, iron, copper, coal, salt, tin, potash and other minerals.

Agriculture and cattle-rearing are the chief industries. The principal livestock are cows, horses, sheep, camels, mules and donkeys. The soil is exceedingly fertile producing corn, wheat, dhourra, barley, rye, peas, cotton, sugar-cane and all kinds of tropical fruit with little cultivation. Coffee grows wild in the provinces of Harrar and Caffa. Ethiopia is the original home of coffee.

Wild animals are abundant. The lion, symbol of Ethiopia, attains its largest size there. There are deer, zebras, wild oxen, elephants, hippopotamuses, rhinoceroses, leopards, hyenas and monkeys of various kinds in myriads. The Ethiopian giraffe is the tallest and finest in the world, and much sought after by zoological gardens. Menelik once used this fact to show his displeasure to nations having an alliance with Italy by forbidding exportations of Ethiopian giraffes to them.

Most varieties of tropical birds are also to be found there, including the ostrich.

There are several curative hot springs, one of the finest being at Addis-Ababa.

The principal exports are coffee, hides, skins and wax. The chief imports are cotton goods. Currency is the heavy Maria Theresa silver thaler, or dollar, which is worth about thirty American cents, though it is almost twice as large as the American dollar. In distant parts of the interior salt is used for small currency.

Ethiopian trade is at present insignificant. Its total imports and exports do not exceed $15,000,000 annually. When properly developed Ethiopia, with her fine climate and enormous natural resources, bids fair to become an earthly paradise.

THE ETHIOPIAN MAN

HE Ethiopians are brave, hardy, of fine physique and inured to war by thousands of years of self-defense. They are very mobile, being perhaps the swifest and most enduring runners on earth. They travel light, their commisseary being almost non-existent. Cattle are driven along with the army, and killed and eaten raw to avoid the enemy's seeing their smoke. Parched grain is carried in a knapsack. Their tents and blankets are mother-earth.

In strategy the African has been renowned since the days of Hannibal of Carthage. In the clash at Walwal, December 5, 1934, the Ethiopian commander drove his cattle against the Italian tanks putting them to confusion as Hannibal did the Romans, or Cetewayo, Zulu king, did the British in 1879.

THE ETHIOPIAN WOMAN

HE Ethiopian woman enjoys a greater degree of independence than those of any other land. She is complete mistress of her body and her property.

She has four kinds of marriage from which to choose. One is a contract for two years, another is a civil union of indeterminate length. If the first is successful it usually leads to the second.

But if it is not she may free herself from either at any time, without expense, merely by calling in a disinterested person to act as judge.

The third is a church marriage. This is usually taken only by couples who through the years have grown to feel that they were made for each other. From this there is no divorce.

In the fourth a woman hires herself as a combination wife and servant by the year. But all these different marriages must be sworn to before a priest and regular witnesses. Naturally as Ethiopia is composed of several peoples, who differ in customs and in religion, there are exceptions to the above.

An Ethiopian woman may bring her husband to court even for calling her a bad name, have him fined, and pocket the fine. And she needs no witnesses as Ethiopian women have the reputation of being the most truthful in the world.

She goes with her husband to war, and often becomes his avenger, should he fall. Usually she is fiercer in battle than the man. Europeans sometimes kill themselves, rather than fall into the hands of the African woman.

Queen Taitu, wife of Menelik, was a famous warrior. She led her own troops to battle against the Italian at Adowa, and spurred on the men by her valiant conduct.

THE SEX LURE OF ETHIOPIA

N addition to the economic there is another lure of the Italians in Ethiopia which cannot be ignored. That is the sex lure—the prospects of having Ethiopian girls. Already novels are appearing in Italy whose heroes are sturdy young Fascisti and whose heroines are beautiful Ethiopians. According to the Associated Press the Fascists in East Africa want to marry the dusky maidens but Mussolini objects.

There are hundred of mulattoes now in Ethiopia by Italian fathers. One of the great attractions that Africa holds for the white man has been the abundance of black women in a nude or semi-nude state, as Mary

Gaunt and other African travellers have said.

The lure of the black woman also played an important part in the American Civil War. David Goodman Croly, a white editor of that time, declared that one of the principal reasons why the Southern men fought to preserve slavery was that they feared that freedom would deprive them of sexual domination over the Negro women.

BRITAIN'S BOND TO ETHIOPIA

THIOPIA is of the first strategic importance to the British Empire. To her east is the Red Sea, which is the life-line of Britain; to her west is the Cape-to-Cairo Railway, aptly described as Britain's spinal cord in Africa; in Ethiopia's centre is Lake Tsana, the source of the Blue Nile as well as the sources of other rivers, which if diverted would make British territory to the north and all Egypt almost a Sahara, or at least as worthless as the Italian possessions in Africa.

In control of Ethiopia, Italy would be a menace to the other white powers already there. By training and arming the warlike Ethiopians she could conquer the surrounding territory; cut off England from India, Australia, and her colonies in the Far East; imperil France on both shores of the Mediterranean; and be dominant in Europe. Mussolini is a far greater menace to world peace than the Kaiser.

Having failed to seize Ethiopia, Britain is now firm for her independence and in all her treaties with England and France regarding Ethiopia has always insisted on this.

WHAT THE ETHIOPIANS MIGHT EXPECT UNDER ITALIAN RULE

HOULD the Italians ever dominate Ethiopia, the Ethiopians may expect the same treatment that the Italians meted out to the natives of Tripoli since 1911. The Tripolitan tribesmen who were as determined to guard their independence as the Ethiopians are, were butchered in a manner unparalleled in modern times. On October 29, 1911, during the Turco-Italian war, 4,000 non-combatants, including women and children were massacred. For a recital of this horror not from one news correspondent, but several, see F. McCullagh's "Italy's War for a Desert", Part IV. "The Massacres", pp. 246-395. Also the N. Y. Times, October 31 and November 1, 1911.

In January, 1932, another appalling butchery occurred. Having built 180 miles of barb wire to hem in the Senussi, the Italians herded, it is said, some fifty thousand of them together, and then showered bombs on them from the air, utterly wiping them out. This atrocity caused the greatest indignation throughout Islam. (N. Y. Times, May 3; December 16, 1931 and January 27, 1932.)

Ruthless at home, Fascism has introduced some new horrors in her colonizing in Africa.

HAILE SELASSIE I
(Power of the Holy Trinity)

AILE SELASSIE I, King of Kings of Ethiopia, last of the independent sovereigns of Africa, and now centre of the world's attention, was born on July 17, 1891, according to the Western calendar, or 1883, according to the Ethiopian one. His father was the Ras Makonnen, a nephew of Menelik, who distinguished himself in the victorious war against Italy in 1896.

Haile Selassie was an extraordinarily bright youth and showed great promise of statesmanship at an early age. At fourteen he was the Governor of Garamoulta, which post he relinquished on the death of his father to reside at the court of Menelik.

There he continued his studies under Ethiopian and European tutors. Then Menelik appointed him governor of Basso which post he filled with such competence that he was made administrator of Harrar, the most important province of Ethiopia, while he was not yet twenty.

At this time he nearly lost his life. While crossing Lake Arumuya with seven others the boat capsized. He swam ashore; the rest were drowned.

As the result of political intrigue he was removed from Harrar and sent to the distant province of Caffa, but thanks to his skill and his integrity he was soon restored to Menelik's favor.

On Menelik's death, Lidj Yassu, Menelik's grandson, came to the throne. Lidj Yassu's father, the Ras Michael, was a Mohammedan, and Lidj Yassu too, showed Islamic sympathies. He took several wives, wore the fez, and sided with the "Mad" Mullah, a Mohammedan prophet, who had driven the British from all of Somaliland save the coast.

Ethiopia's policy for 1,600 years has been a Christian one. As the King of England pledges himself to maintain Protestantism so the Emperor of Ethiopia must swear to uphold Christianity. Lidj Yassu by his observance of Mohammedan customs was thus violating Ethiopian law.

During the war of 1914, Lidj Yassu also sided with Germany and tried to bring about a union of Christian and Mohammedan against England and her allies. Since Ethiopia is of strategic importance to Britain the maintenance of Christianity in Ethiopia and her friendliness to England are of vital political importance to the welfare of the British empire. Hostility to Britain might have meant war against Ethiopia. Therefore the Abuna, or head of the Ethiopian church, and the Ethiopian leaders deposed Lidj Yassu. In his place they put Zauditu, or Judith, a daughter of Menelik, Haile Selassie (then the Ras Tafari) was named heir to the throne and regent.

Lidj Yassu's father, the Ras Michael, gathered a large army and marched against the Christians. In a great battle fought at Sagalle on October 27, 1916, the Ras Michael was totally defeated. Haile Selassie, who was one of the Christian commanders, distinguished himself by his generalship and his valor.

When Lidj Yassu gathered another army in 1921, Haile Selassie marched against him, captured him, and held him prisoner, which he still is.

In 1923, Haile Selassie again showed his statesmanship by maneouvering himself into the League of Nations, despite the opposition of England, Australia, Holland, Norway and Lithuania, but with the support of France, Italy, Portugal, Belgium and the Latin-American nations. Hereafter none of the European powers would be able to absorb Ethiopia without breaking

Above: Belaten Gheta Herouy, Foreign Minister; H. R. H., the Duke of Glou-
ter; the interpreter, son of the Foreign Minister; H. M. Haile Selassie; and Gen.
rgine, at Addis-Ababa. (Photo by the author.)
Below: Haile Selassie; Lidj Yassu, deposed Emperor; and Ras Birru, who is
v on a mission to Japan.

the Covenant of the League. The great wisdom of this move is now being demonstrated.

In 1924 he toured Europe with an imposing retinue of thirty Rases, or princes, with their trains. Some of these were his secret enemies, who were plotting to take his place, and he took them along so that he could keep his eyes on them.

In England he was received by King George at Buckingham Palace and dined there. Cambridge University conferred on him the degree of LL.D. King Albert of Belgium, Victor Emmanuel of Italy, the President of France, and other rulers received him with the honors due the heir to a throne.

On his return to Ethiopia he tried to modernise the ancient empire. He introduced the telephone, and the airship; built a wireless station and sent promising Ethiopian youths to be trained in France, Germany, England. and the United States, looking forward to the day when the great natural resources of Ethiopia would be developed by her own mechanics, engineers, scientists, and aviators. In these efforts he worked from sixteen to eighteen hours a day—a great feat in a hot climate. He knew that in order to win. the sympathy and good will of the world he must head off the charge that he was permitting rich territory fit for "white" habitation to remain in a backward state.

In addition he took steps to modernise the form of government from the old patriarchal one, and remodelled the police and the army.

All of this was done under great opposition from the Empress and her party. The latter held that the old customs were good enough, hoping by the preservation of them to curb European influence which has proved so disastrous to the freedom of the African peoples. Haile Selassie, on the other hand, thought it was possible to adopt beneficial European customs and inventions, and at the same time keep European influence within bounds. Perhaps he would prefer even less of this as he has said, "We need European progress only because we are surrounded by it. That is at once a benefit and a misfortune."

In 1928, the leaders of Ethiopia in recognition of his services appointed him Negus, or King, and he was crowned in October of that year. Nominal power still remained in the hands of the Empress Zaiditu. That same year he concluded a treaty of perpetual peace with Italy.

In 1930, the Ras Guksa, the husband of the Empress revolted. Haile Selassie marched against him, and defeated him, the Ras Guksa being among the slain.

The news of her husband's death killed Zaiditu and Haile Selassie succeeded to the throne, and was crowned amid great ceremonies and festivity at Addis-Ababa on November 2, 1930. Among those present at the coronation were the Duke of Gloucester, son of George V; the Duke of the Udine, nephew of Victor Emmanuel of Italy; and the Marshal Franchet d'Esperey of France.

But the accession to full power gave Haile Selassie by no means a free hand to carry out his reforms. He had first of all to contend with the great Rases, or rulers of provinces, who were as jealous of their power as the various states of the American union are of theirs. Some of the chiefs were subject only in name, and were actually hostile, while the lack of roads and communications made it impossible for the emperor to check them at short notice. Wild tribesmen profited by these, too, to invade the territory of adjoining nations, thus bringing reproach on the central power, and causing the payments of indemnities.

Another internal obstacle was the swarming Ethiopian clergy, which is very powerful, and ultra-conservative, and eager to keep the people in ignorance to serve its own ends. The venality, and superstition of this clergy is amazing. Today, like the clergy of the Middle Ages it opposes all scientific innovation and progress and even modern methods of healing.

Haile Selassie also had to contend with incessant foreign intrigue for the economic control, and even the direct seizure, of his country that went on not only abroad but in Ethiopia itself.

His economic difficulties were tremendous. Ethiopia, though rich in natural resources, is yet in the stage of primitive agriculture. Her coinage, such as Haile Selassie found it, was unstable and being of silver was of small value in the purchase of modernising implements in the gold countries. Further, such reforms are usually effected by foreign loans, but Ethiopian policy is not to borrow abroad. Haile Selassie knows that the first step towards losing his independence would be to owe money to Europe or America. Money to carry out his reforms has been and still is his great handicap.

Yet working under these and other disadvantages, he has instituted a Parliament and modern courts, has built roads, hospitals, schools, installed electric lighting in the streets, improved the commerce and international relations, all the while steering a diplomatic course between opposing factions and religions in his own land.

As for his daily duties they are manifold. He receives the diplomats of the various nations, attends to some minute details of the government or the army; gives orders and inspects the erection of a building or the installation of machinery, and the like, all in addition to being the chief justice of the empire. Each subject, however lowly, has the right of direct appeal to the Emperor. In the meantime he keeps an almost housewifely eye for other details. Passing along in his red Rolls Royce he will sometimes descend to instruct the Gouragi road-workers and might lift a stone, himself, to put it in the proper place. Truly he is the guiding spirit of his nation in the fullest sense of the word. He is the rare spectacle nowadays of the monarch being the greatest in the land not only in name but in worth, ability, and vision. Even more than Mussolini, he is the maker of his country.

As one writer has said, "The weight of the whole empire rests upon the shoulders of this quiet but iron-hearted little sovereign.

"Night and day he is beset by a thousand different problems and a thousand different worries and perplexities. Even while he eats he transacts state business. Even while he sleeps he has no respite.

"His secretary sleeps at the foot of his majesty's bed, ready at any moment to take the Emperor's orders in the event his majesty awakens and thinks about something he had forgotten during the day.

"Under terrific strain, he is trying almost overnight to transform his medieval empire into a modern state."

Astonishment will increase when it is known that like Napoleon and Ghandi, he is a small man. Haile Selassie is barely over five feet tall, and weighs, it seems, not over a hundred and twenty pounds.

Haile Selassie's outstanding accomplishment, however, has been his fight against slavery, which had existed in Ethiopia from time immemorial. He began by freeing all the slaves in his palace; after which he made laws for the gradual emancipation of the remainder in the empire. He provided free education and clothing for the children of slaves and ex-slaves, together with appointment to government posts, depending upon individual ability; founded an anti-slavery society and an anti-slavery court; and made slave-raiding punishable with death. In 1935 he issued a proclamation wiping out slavery forever. In all his reforms Haile Selassie has had to go slow. He cannot change the psychology of his people or educate them overnight. One recalls the fate of King Amanuallah of Afghanistan, who tried to hasten progress in his own land. Moreover, most of Haile Selassie's people are anti-European in their ways. They know that the Europeans are ever scheming to take away their land as they did all the rest of Africa.

In disposition he is firm. His countrymen call him "Arko" (The Vise) for when he believes he is right he stands firm. In March, 1935, when Mussolini demanded a diplomatic apology, an indemnity, and the saluting of the Italian flag at Addis-Ababa over the Walwal incident, Haile Selassie sent him a flat refusal. And he did the unprecedented thing of giving out his reply to the press before he gave it to Italy thus giving Mussolini no chance to make it appear otherwise to the Italian people.

When George Bernard Shaw suggested that he yield to Italy and become a protectorate, he replied.

"I would rather kill myself, like Emperor Theodore sixty years ago, than become a puppet prince under the Italians

"I would be unworthy of my great ancestors, beginning with Solomon, if I submitted to Italian vassalage. Nor can I, as Sovereign of the oldest empire in the world, which had its beginnings before the Flood, accept a British protectorate or an Anglo-French regime.

"We cannot cut up Ethiopia like a cake, handing sugared parts to this and that country just to win their smiles and satisfy their sweet tooth.

"Would England or any other sovereign nation give up territory so willingly? No! I have taken an oath to the memory of the great Menelik to defend the empire until God calls me unto Him."

In manners, Haile Selassie is pleasing and most affable, yet full of dignity. His face radiates intelligence, serenity, kindliness, good nature and immense reserves of power. He smiles frequently, seeming at all times perfectly at ease. A Christian at heart, he observes the high principles of that faith. When a man who had tried to assassinate him was sentenced to death, Haile Selassie not only refused to sign the warrant, but forgave him. He has also abolished public hangings; mutilation for habitual thieves; and is endeavoring to supplant the old Mosaic law by which a murderer is handed over to the victim's next of kin, with modern law. But it is also said that he never forgets an enemy.

In features he is Oriental, a fact accentuated by his beard. In color he is a lightish black-brown, and considerably darker than one would infer from the published pictures of him. In reality he is what one would call in the United States a dark mulatto, judged both by his color and his hair. In his general expression he has been aptly described by one writer as a "black edition of the pictured Christ."

In his family life Haile Selassie differs from most Oriental monarchs; he has no concubines and only one wife. In 1912 he married Weyzero Menen, who has borne him five children. The Empress is a great granddaughter of Menelik, and a niece of the deposed emperor.

HOW DO THE ETHIOPIANS FEEL
TOWARDS THE AFRAMERICANS ?

UT the Ethiopians do not consider themselves Negroes, many Aframericans will say. This is true. They object to the word, and so for that matter do many Aframericans, not to mention the Aframericans south of the Rio Grande, who do not use it.

A leading Ethiopian once said to this writer, "We think of ourselves as a nation, not as a race. This does not mean that we do not recognise our kinship with peoples of African descent in the New World. We wish you would urge as many as possible of your skilled farmers, mechanics, and scientists to come to Ethiopia. We need them here and would give them land free."

Ethiopia has always shown her friendliness to such Aframericans as have visited her. Menelik had a black West Indian, Dr. Vitalien, as his personal physician and adviser. He warmly welcomed Sylvain, the Haitian poet, and Daniel R. Alexander, a missionary, who still resides at Addis-Ababa.

Three different missions to the United States tried to get trained Aframericans in vain.

In 1930 Haile Selassie appointed Dr. J. B. West of Washington, D. C., as his personal physician. He gave Hubert Julian a large sum of money, made him a colonel in his army, and conferred on him the Gold Order of Menelik. He has made John Robinson of Chicago one of his principal aviators, and is using Aframerican world war veterans as drill-masters.

Lastly in one of his declarations Haile Selassie has announced that he is the head not only of Ethiopia, but of all peoples of African descent everywhere.

Aframericans in Ethiopia will be well-received provided that they do not go there with airs of superiority, and that they remember that the Ethiopians, never having been under white domination, look upon themselves exactly as white Americans or Englishmen do themselves in their own land.

Besides there will be a mutual economic benefit for both Aframericans and Ethiopians. The Ethiopians lack education and training and are hungering for it, preferably from teachers of their own color. The Aframerican needs an outlet for his trained youth. And if the economic depression lasts in America opportunities for skilled Negroes will become increasingly less. Ethiopia offers a vast outlet for Aframerican energies and Negro youths need have no longer any hesitancy in training themselves in engineering and other mechanical sciences.

Amharic, the official Ethiopian language, should be taught in Negro schools. Skilled Negroes should form a society in order to arrange for employment with the Ethiopian government.

HAILE SELASSIE AND MUSSOLINI CONTRASTE[

OTHING could be more striking than the difference between Haile Selassie and Mussolini

Mussolini glorifies war. His method of settling with a rival is to threaten him, and if that fails, kill him. Haile Selassie cultivates peace. His way of removing a rival is by conciliation. Born to autocratic power, Haile Selassie has voluntarily relinquished it, and is endeavoring to make Ethiopia a democracy. Mussolini, born under a constitutional monarchy, and once a Socialist, himself, has turned his country into an autocracy worse than under any sultan or czar. Haile Selassie belongs to the oldest family in the world, royal or otherwise. He is descended from King Ori of 4470 B. C. He can name all the rulers, his ancestors, who came after Ori. Despite this super-aristocratic lineage and the fact that he is invested with power more absolute than Mussolini was able to seize, he is modest, quiet, unassuming, affable and utterly without pose.

This writer has observed Haile Selassie for hours at a time—at military reviews, at the races, at public ceremonies, in his palace—and it has struck him that Haile Selassie in his every move was a gentleman-born, a true aristocrat.

Mussolini, on the other hand, is the direct descendant of a family that has been peasants for three centuries. His father was a blacksmith. He, himself, was a poor school-master, who through his ability rose to supreme power in his native land. While we know that character, not birth, is the principal force in the making of great men and that servants sometimes make able and considerate masters, Mussolini exhibits all the odious traits of the servant who has risen to authority, against which we are warned in the Bible. He is a strutter, poseur, braggart, and breather of defiance. His every move and gesture is calculated to impress the rabble. He is perpetually showing off. As Abdullah, King of Transjordania, recently said: "Mussolini's manner of speaking and the way he appears in photographs make me imagine him to be a cheap comedian."

This writer has also watched Mussolini in action at the Palazzio Venezia in Rome—shooting up his hand, pouting, grimacing, puffing out cheeks like a porcupine fish, gesturing, and otherwise clowning.

Great events would seem at times to prepare and train the men that are to handle them. For the American Revolution there was a Washington and for the Civil War a Lincoln. What might have happened to America but for these men? So it is with Ethiopia. The hand of destiny through difficult mazes brought Haile Selassie to supreme power. There were others, who were nearer to the throne than he. Now he stands forth as a wise and peerless leader. He is not only the foremost Ethiopian, but the leading individual of African descent. Indeed, it is not too much to say that he is the foremost living statesman.

In his address to Parliament on July 18, 1935, he said:

"We have always believed that a government ennobles, not debases itself when it voluntarily submits a quarrel to the judgment, perhaps the condemnation, of a qualified impartial international body."

Here is a model for all future statesmen to follow. With such an attitude wars will be no more. Thousands of years ago Ethiopia gave to the world the first ideal of right and wrong—the first morality. Today across the dim centuries Haile Selassie again points the way to interracial and international amity and brotherhood, which is the true goal of civilisation.

For a list of the Ethiopian kings from Ori of 4470 B. C. to Haile Selassie, see: Rey, C. F. In the Country of the Blue Nile, pp. 263-274, London, 1927.

Above: Her Majesty, the Empress Menen.　Below: The Emperor's retreat at Bishoftou.

WHAT ARE ETHIOPIA'S CHANCES
OF VICTORY

WE refrain purposely from making any prediction as to Ethiopia's chances of success in a war with Italy. Ethiopia has an estimated total of 1,160,000 fighting men of whom only 237,000 have any degree of modern training. The latter are disposed as follows: the army of Ras Kassa of Beghie-Medir, 50,000; of Ras Emerou of Godjam, 50,000; of Ras Nessibu of Harrar, 20,000; of the Crown Prince, Asfa Wosen, 40,000; and the well-trained Imperial Guard of 7,000.

But Ethiopia has allies against which tanks, airplanes, and poison-gas will be useless. They are sun-stroke; burning, waterless deserts; towering peaks; gorges and ravines a mile deep; no roads; wide rivers to be bridged; sand storms; lack of sanitary drinking water; poisoned wells; tropical downpours that make the ground as slippery as soap; insects, whose bites cause irritation, disease, and death; malaria and other tropical maladies; and the pressure of the high altitudes.

If the Ethiopians adopt guerilla tactics the heavy armament of the Italians will lack the important objective for which such force was designed. It will be like using an elephant-gun to shoot a mosquito or a giant his full strength to throw a feather. As in the war against Abdel-Krim in Morocco, airplanes will serve chiefly in removing the wounded, while the heavy metal containers used for poison gas will prove largely to be but so much impedimenta. The Italians took twenty-one years (1911-1932) to subdue the desert tribes of Cyrenaica, who were less than 230,000, were much nearer home, and on less difficult terrain.

In a long war Ethiopia's great peril may be lack of food. She has never had cause to lay in a supply. She has now an estimate of 21,000,000 head of cattle. But the Italians will undoubtedly use their airplanes to destroy the Ethiopian grain-fields and herds.

Ethiopia, Conquering Lion of the Tribe of Judah, saw the rise and the fall of the Pharaohs. She saw the empires of Cambyses, Darius, Cyrus and Alexander the Great melt into nothingness. She saw the glory that was Greece and the grandeur that was Rome become heaps of stone. This most ancient of the nations saw the rising and the setting of the Caesars of the West and of the East. She saw the birth of Islam, witnessed its sweep across the entire Old World, and aided in its check. She saw the rise and decline of, the Holy Roman Empire and the discovery of the New World. She saw black men become slaves in the New World and again win their freedom. She beheld the rise and the fall of Portugal, Spain, Holland, Sweden; was present at Napoleon's rise to power and his eclipse; as also that of the German Kaiser. She played the leading role in the downfall of two previous Mussolinis—Depretis and Crispi—and by the aid of her strong right arm and dauntless spirit she will also see the discomfiture and disgrace of this latest menace to world peace and brotherhood—Mussolini.

FOR GENERAL READING

Rey, C. F.—Unconquered Abyssinia, London, 1923.
Gruehl, M.—Citadel of Ethiopia, London, 1932.
Baum, J. E.—Savage Abyssinia, London, 1927.
Walker, C. H.—The Abyssinian at Home, London, 1933.
McCreagh, G.—The last of free Africa.
Gruehl, M.—Citadel of Ethiopia, London, 1932.
Nesbitt, L.—The Hell Hole of Creation, N. Y. 1932.

ETHIOPIA'S CHIEF NEED

IF civilization is a necessity of Ethiopia then Haile Selassie is by far the most logical leader of his own people, and Mussolini the least. In the present state of mind of the Ethiopians, the Italians will find no co-operation and must use coercion. Moreover, if the abolition of slavery is Italy's goal, she has failed in this respect in her North African colonies. In April, 1935, she was forced to admit at the League of Nations that slavery existed in Libya. Her report said, "In the zones controlled by us it was not possible, however, to extirpate the residual form of slavery that subsisted—essentially slavery of a domestic character. The old slaves continued to live in the families in which they already were, some of them refusing to leave their former masters . . .

"The present situation as regards domestic servitude is uniform throughout the colony . . .

"These remnants of domestic slavery will gradually disappear." (League of Nations Publications. Slavery. I. B.1, pp. 100-101).

In short this sounds like the same promises that Haile Selassie are making to get rid of slavery if given time.

It is true that the Amhara, or ruling class, has been oppressive—a condition that the Emperor is striving hard to correct. But if the Italians ever take control, the oppressed will have cause to long for the good old days of paternal slavery. As the New York Post says editorially:

"Fishing, farming and hunting are still free. So it is not economically necessary for the natives to work for a few pennies a day for some great Italian corporation. Italy, if it conquers Ethiopia, will remedy this. The farm land will be taken away from the peasants. Prohibitive taxes will be put on fishing and hunting. Slavery will no longer be necessary. Ethiopians will have to work or starve, and their masters will be relieved of the obligation to feed them when there is no work.

"Just as in civilized Italy."

Given the money, Haile Selassie and his people seem perfectly capable of working out their own salvation, and establishing the form of civilization best adapted to their country.

270421-300-11-60W

www.ingramcontent.com/pod-product-compliance
Lightning Source LLC
Chambersburg PA
CBHW071801020426
42331CB00008B/2354